To Blanche, Rhett, Jennings, Charlotte and Davis...
If trees could talk, what stories would they tell us? Enjoy this tree's story!

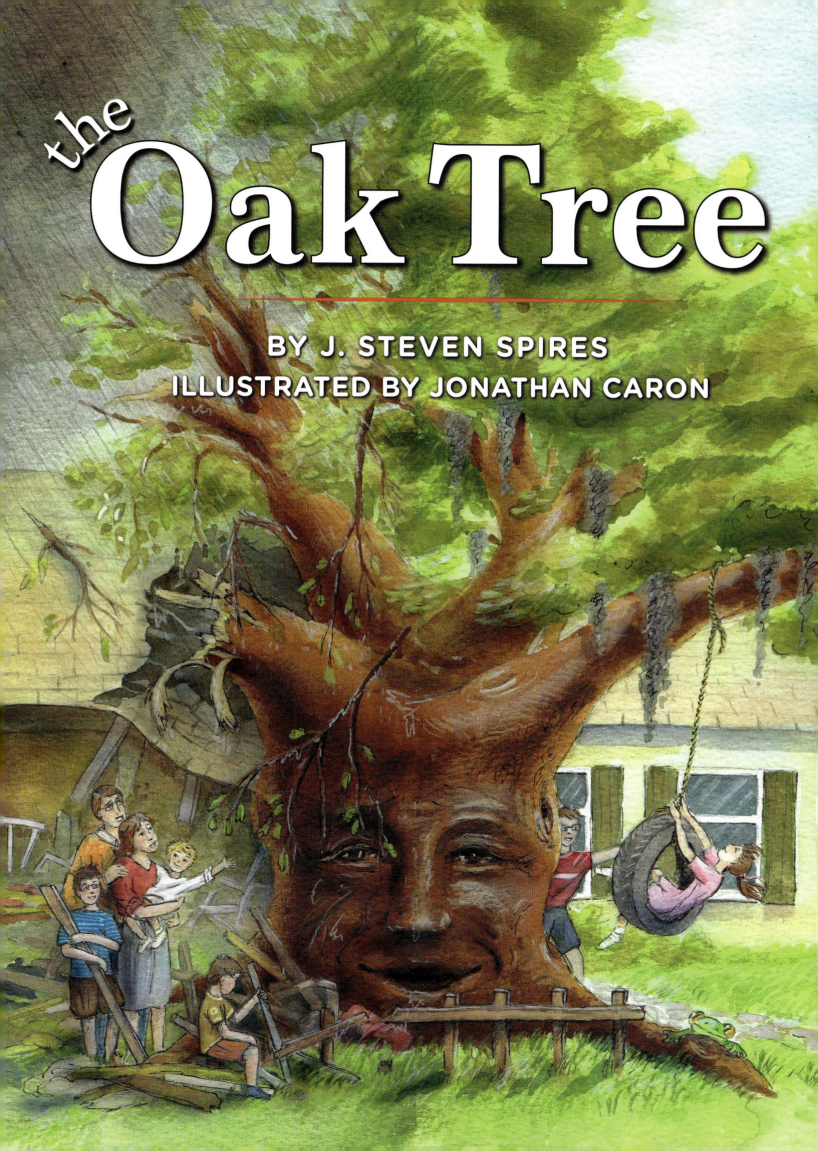

the Oak Tree

Text copyright © 2015 by J. Steven Spires
Illustrations copyright © 2015 by Jonathan Caron

All rights reserved. No part of this publication may be reproduced, stored in a retrieval system, or transmitted in any form or by any means - electronic, mechanical, photocopy, recording or any other - except for brief quotations in printed reviews, without the prior permission of the publisher.

For more information, address:
Inspired Books Publishing
112 North Dabney Drive
Slidell, LA 70458
www.inspiredbookspublishing.com

Book design by Rachel Guillot / reguillo1025@gmail.com

Publisher's Cataloging-in-Publication Data

Spires, J. Steven.
The oak tree / written by J. Steven Spires; illustrated by Jonathan Caron.
"p" cm.
ISBN: 978-0-9858469-4-7 (hardcover)
ISBN: 978-0-9858469-5-4 (pbk)
1. Oak—fiction. 2. Trees—Fiction. 3. Hurricanes—Fiction. 4. Hurricane Katrina, 2005—Fiction.   I. Caron, Jonathan, illustrator. II. Title.
PZ7.1.S65 Oak 2015   [Fic]—dc23   2015903014

Printed in the United States of America
First Edition 10 9 8 7 6 5 4 3 2 1

First printing in July, 2015

For the survivors and the families of victims
of Hurricanes Katrina, Rita and other natural disasters,
who have lost everything but remained resilient and have
come back even stronger. – J.S.S.

For all fathers,
who through whatever crises may arise,
will always lead us to a safer haven. – J.C.

The new day has just begun. A warm sun hangs over a house. No one is up yet and the house is very still.

Near the house an old oak tree stands. Its branches touch the morning sky.

Tweet, tweet!

Chirrup, chirrup!

The early birds land first, awakening the tree. Some sing a song. Others hunt small bugs.

A man in a suit steps out of the house. "Goodbye, dear family," the man says. He gives everyone a hug. "It's time for me to go to work."

The man gets in his car and starts up the engine.

vROOOOOOOM!

The children smile and wave. The mom watches the car drive away. The house is alive now.

Nearby a little one is learning to walk. He toddles slowly. His mom follows after him. He stops to look at the oak tree.

Along comes a neighbor hobbling with a cane. "It's so hot," he complains. "Thank goodness for this oak tree's shade."

"Twee, twee," the little one says. They both look at the oak tree and smile.

The old tree can't help but smile too.

The mom picks up the little boy and hugs him, "Time for a nap," she says. The neighbor walks on.

The other children play a game of hide-and-seek around the tree. "Ha, ha! Hee, hee! You can't catch me!" they scream.

The oak tree's smile widens.

Chitter-chatter, chitter-chatter

The mom comes back outside and looks to the sky. Dark clouds are gathering. She talks on and on to a friend on the phone.

In the early afternoon, the man returns. The mom and children run to him. They all look unhappy. The little one cries.

A steady wind blows. The oak tree knows a storm is coming. It begins to worry about the family.

Soon, the family quickly packs their van. Meanwhile, the man and his son nail boards on all the windows.

A sudden gust of wind pushes the oak tree's branches up, then down.

BANG-bang-clatter-TWANG!
BANG-bang-clatter-TWANG!

The clouds are heavy now. "Uh-oh, here comes the rain," calls the mom. The oak tree's concern grows.

Two of the children run to the oak tree and hug its trunk. "We'll be back soon!" they promise.

Plip Plop!

Plip Plop!

Everyone then climbs into the van and drives off. The oak tree stands alone and watches the family disappear from view. Its limbs droop.

Time passes slowly and the rain falls harder. Small puddles turn into streams and water covers the ground.

Splat!

The storm grows stronger as heavy rains flood streets and ditches. Still, the oak tree stands tall, remembering the family's promise to return.

Splatter!

Splash!

Throughout the night, gale winds bend the oak tree back and forth. Branches and limbs snap and drop. The oak tree's roots begin to lose their grip. The tree holds on for dear life, while clinging to the children's promise and searching the night.

A new day brings no relief. Flood waters surround the tree. Tired and broken, the oak tree turns toward the family home. Only a tattered roof remains in sight! The house is completely flooded! The hope of a joyful family reunion floats away with the storm debris.

The next morning, birds land on the oak tree. Some are singing a morning song. Others hunt for bugs.

Chirp! Chirp!

Tweet! Tweet!

The day slowly passes. The entire neighborhood sits underwater. Rescue helicopters and airplanes fly about the sky.

Men arrive in small boats and knock on the windows of the family's home. Tap! Tap! Rap! "Is anyone in there?" they shout.

GRRRRRR!

The oak tree listens, but cannot bear to look. No one answers, so an "X" is painted on the outside wall. The boat moves on to the next house.

Whup! Whup! Whup!

The oak tree sits in a silent world for weeks. Then, one day, people begin returning to the neighborhood. Their sounds fill the silence. Some are hugging and crying as they search through the debris. Others move and pile storm garbage in their front yards. As people pass by, the oak tree searches for its family.

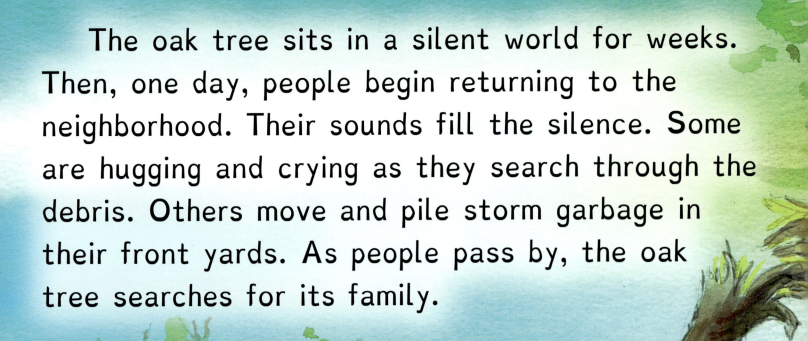

Two workers walk past the oak tree. "This poor old tree," one worker says.

His partner nods and replies, "It almost looks like it's missing someone."

The oak tree sighs.

Next, familiar voices fill the air, "Hello, old friend! We're back! We missed you!"

A feeling of love fills the emptiness brought by the storm.

When the new day begins, a warm sun hangs over a newly framed house and trailer. No one is up yet, and all is still.

Nearby, an oak tree stands. Its tattered branches reach to touch the sky.